What's On Your Plate?

Lunch

Ted and Lola Schaefer

www.raintreepublishers.co.uk
Visit our website to find out more information about **Raintree** books.

To order:
☎ Phone 44 (0) 1865 888066
📄 Send a fax to 44 (0) 1865 314091
💻 Visit the Raintree Bookshop at www.raintreepublishers.co.uk
to browse our catalogue and order online.

First published in Great Britain by Raintree, Halley Court, Jordan Hill, Oxford, OX2 8EJ, part of Harcourt Education.
Raintree is a registered trademark of Harcourt Education Ltd.

Editorial: Patrick Catel, Rosie Gordon and Melanie Waldron
Design: Philippa Jenkins, Lucy Owen, and John Walker
Picture Research: Melissa Allison
Production: Chloe Bloom

Originated by Chroma Graphics (Overseas) Pte Ltd.
Printed and bound in China by South China Printing Company

13-digit ISBN: 978 1 4062 0256 4
10-digit ISBN: 1 406 20256 8
10 09 08 07 06
10 9 8 7 6 5 4 3 2 1

British Library Cataloguing in Publication Data:
Schaefer, Lola M., 1950-
Lunch (What's On Your Plate?)
1. Luncheons - Juvenile literature 2. Natural foods - Juvenile literature 3. Nutrition - Juvenile literature
I. Title II. Schaefer, Ted, 1948-
641.3'02

A full catalogue record for this book is available from the British Library.

Acknowledgements
The publishers would like to thank the following for permission to reproduce photographs:
pp. 18, 26, Corbis; **p. 6,** Corbis/Charles Gupton; **p. 19,** Corbis/Lester Lefkowitz; **p. 14,** Corbis/Lew Robertson; **p. 16,** Creatas; **p. 5,** Getty Images; **p. 27,** Getty Images/Photonica; **pp. 4, 5, 9, 10, 12, 13, 20, 21, 23, 24, 28, 29,** Harcourt Education Ltd/MM Studios; **p. 22,** Harcourt Education Ltd/Tudor Photography; **pp. 17, 25,** PhotoEdit; **p. 15,** PhotoEdit/David Young-Wolff; **p. 7,** PhotoEdit/Mark Richards; **p. 5,** Photolibrary.com

Cover photograph of a sandwich reproduced with permission of Getty Images/Stone/Chris Everard.

The publishers would like to thank Dr Sarah Schenker for her assistance in the preparation of this book.

Dedicated to the memory of Lucy Owen

Contents

Any words appearing in bold, **like this**, are explained in the Glossary.

What is lunch?

Lunch is the meal you eat in the middle of the day. You probably don't need a clock to tell you that it is lunchtime. You have used all the **energy** from your breakfast and you feel hungry! Food is the fuel that keeps you going, and lunch gives you a new supply.

sandwich

tortilla

yoghurt

vegetables

vegetable soup

fruit salad

chicken and rice

Did you eat one of these
for lunch this week?

crab salad, crackers, and fresh fruit are a favourite lunch in Trinidad.

In the UK, many children like a cheese sandwich, a bowl of tomato soup, and grapes.

People often eat flatbread and lentil dhal with a glass of sweetened buttermilk called lassi for lunch in India.

Sweet potato soup and flatbread, with fried banana afterwards, make a good lunch in Peru.

Why do you eat lunch?

A healthy lunch gives your body the **nutrition** you need for the afternoon. Some foods help you grow and stay healthy, while others give you **energy** to play, work, or think.

The amount of energy in food is measured in **kilojoules** or calories. Different foods give your body different amounts.

A good lunch gives you energy for the afternoon.

This chart shows some lunch foods and the amount of energy they supply.

food	kilojoules	(calories)
bowl of vegetable soup	477	(114)
2 slices wholemeal toast	1732	(414)
1 tbsp cottage cheese	330	(79)
apple	197	(47)

tbsp = tablespoons

Your body is using energy all the time whether you are moving or sitting still. Activities that make you feel tired or out of breath use more calories. Running uses more energy than walking.

This bar chart is a guide to the amount of kilojoules (kJ) your body may use during these activities.

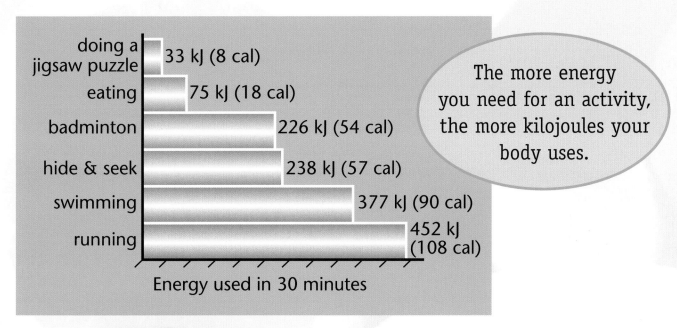

doing a jigsaw puzzle — 33 kJ (8 cal)
eating — 75 kJ (18 cal)
badminton — 226 kJ (54 cal)
hide & seek — 238 kJ (57 cal)
swimming — 377 kJ (90 cal)
running — 452 kJ (108 cal)

Energy used in 30 minutes

The more energy you need for an activity, the more kilojoules your body uses.

Quiz
How many kilojoules would you use while swimming for one hour?

(Answer at the bottom of the page)

Answer: You would need 754 kJ (180 cal) to swim for one hour.

What are the healthiest lunch foods?

The foods you choose for lunch can be part of a healthy **diet**. A diet is what you eat each day. A diet can be healthy or unhealthy, because not all foods give you the same **nutrients**.

The food groups needed for a healthy diet are shown in this chart.

You need to eat the right amounts of lots of different foods to give your body all the **nutrition** it needs.

FRUIT & VEGETABLES

BREAD, OTHER CEREALS & POTATOES

MEAT, FISH & ALTERNATIVES

FOODS CONTAINING FAT & SUGAR

MILK & DAIRY FOODS

The chart above shows that some food groups should make up a smaller amount of your daily diet. If you use this chart, you can make sure that you get the food balance right.

Lunch can include foods from each group. A cheese sandwich includes the "bread, other cereals, and potatoes" group, and the "milk and dairy foods" group. Add a bowl of vegetable and bean soup and some grapes to make a complete meal. These foods contain all the fat and sugar you need. Choosing good foods will help you feel strong and healthy.

This lunch has foods from each group. It is healthy, tasty and easy to make.

Lunch foods and nutrition

All food contains **nutrients** that are needed by your body for different things. Some nutrients like **carbohydrates, proteins, and fats** give you **energy**. Nutrients like **vitamins** and **minerals** are needed for health. Protein is also needed for growth, and repairing injuries.

Which lunch foods give you these nutrients?

Carbohydrates

Proteins

Fats

Vitamins are needed by every part of your body. They keep your skin and eyes healthy and make your **immune system** strong. Your immune system helps you get better when you are ill or injured, and prevents you from getting sick.

Minerals, like calcium and phosphorus, are used by your body to build strong bones and teeth. Minerals also help your blood and nerves to work.

vitamin A
vitamin B
potassium

Fresh vegetables, like tomatoes, are packed with nutrients. Your body needs these to stay healthy and grow.

Vitamins and minerals needed for a healthy body

vitamins: vitamins A, B, C, D, E, and K.
minerals: calcium, potassium, iron, zinc, magnesium, and phosphorus.

minerals and water

11

Bread, other cereals, and potatoes for lunch

"Bread, other cereals, and potatoes" is an important food group. These are the best foods to give your body **carbohydrates**. You need these for energy. They also contain **vitamins**, **minerals**, and **fibre**.

You should always choose at least one food from this group as part of your lunch. Vary your choices each day.

Pasta is made from flour from cereal grains. It contains carbohydrates, which give you energy for a long time.

Lunch around the world

In Japan, children sometimes eat triangle-shaped rice cakes for lunch. On the outside they are crisp. Inside, there is a savoury filling.

Grains like wheat, rice, and oats are used to make different foods, like oat cakes, bread, pasta and rice cakes. Some grains are **milled** into white flour, to make white bread or pasta. This removes some of the **fibre**. Wholegrain foods have more fibre. You can include both types in a healthy diet. Foods with fibre help keep your **gut** healthy.

Foods made from grains come in many shapes and sizes. Are there any here that you haven't tried yet?

Fruit and vegetables for lunch

5-A-DAY
Eat at least 5 portions of fruit and vegetables each day

Fruit and vegetables are full of the **nutrients** you need for good health. They give your body **vitamins, minerals, carbohydrates,** and **fibre**. A good **diet** includes fruit and vegetables every day.

You can put lots of fruit and vegetables in a salad. This gives you lots of vitamins and minerals.

Eating fresh vegetables in a sandwich or wrap is a tasty way to get good nutrition for lunch.

Veggie wrap

Always ask an adult to help you in the kitchen.

1. Spread a flour tortilla with cream cheese.
2. Place avocado, cucumber and tomato slices over half the tortilla.
3. Place four leaves of lettuce on the tomato.
4. Sprinkle crunchy chopped onion or beansprouts on top.
5. Roll up firmly.

Fruit and vegetables give you a variety of vitamins and minerals. Eat many different kinds for a healthy diet.

More fruit and vegetables!

Eating fruits and vegetables is a very good way to get vitamin C. You need this for a healthy **immune system**. Vitamin C is not stored in your body, so you need to make sure you get some from fruit and vegetables every day.

Watermelon has no fat and is high in fibre and vitamins A and C. It also has the mineral potassium.

All types of fruit and vegetables count towards your 5-a-day target. You can include fresh, frozen, or canned fruit and vegetables. You can have dried fruit like apricots and raisins, or natural, unsweetened juices and smoothies.

Most shops have a wide variety of fresh fruits any time of the year.

Lunch around the world

India grows more bananas than any other country in the world. Some bananas are sliced and fried to make banana wafers. Some children in India like to eat banana wafers with their lunch.

17

Healthy milk and dairy foods for lunch

Foods in the "milk and dairy foods" group are important to include in your diet, because they give you calcium. Calcium is a **mineral** needed for healthy teeth and bones.

Milk and dairy foods also provide **protein**, **vitamins**, and other minerals, such as phosphorous and magnesium. These are also important for strong teeth and bones.

A glass of milk is a good source of calcium.

Dairy foods can be made with many kinds of milk. Different people around the world drink the milk from cows, goats, sheep, horses, camels, reindeer, and water buffalo. All these milks are healthy because they contain calcium and protein. Foods such as yoghurt and cheese have the same **nutrients** as the milk they are made from.

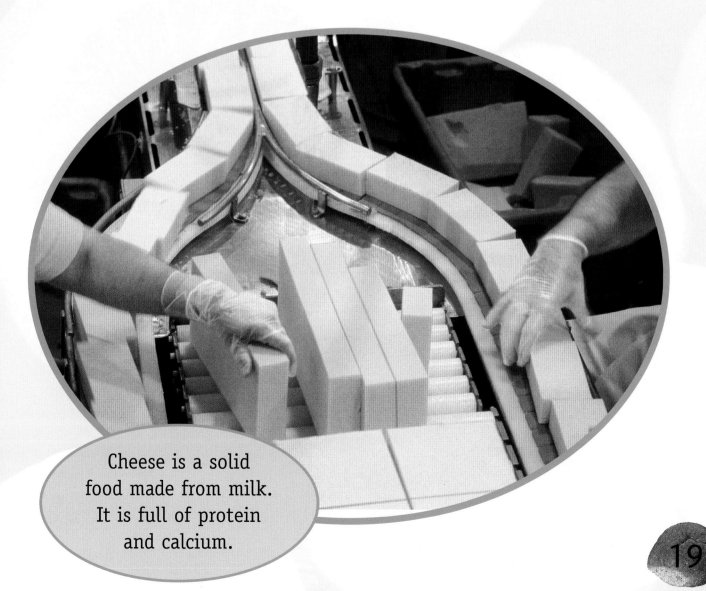

Cheese is a solid food made from milk. It is full of protein and calcium.

Meat, fish, and alternatives for lunch

The "meat, fish, and alternatives" group includes meat, fish, beans, nuts, seeds, soya, and eggs. These foods are all together because they give you **protein**. Proteins are needed for growth and healing. They include **amino acids**, which are needed to make your body's new **cells**. Everything in your body is made of tiny cells put together in different ways.

As your nails grow, new cells are made under the skin, and you trim off old cells when you cut your nails. Protein is needed for healthy new cells.

The foods in this group also contain minerals and fats.

Meat supplies the protein you need but it can also be high in fat. Choose **lean** meats and lower fat meat products for a healthier **diet**.

75g lean beef burger
+ 50g mixed grain bun
+ mustard
+ ketchup
= 1544 kilojoules (369 calories) and 18g of fat

g = grams

75g smoked white turkey
+ 2 slices wholemeal bread
+ 2 tsp low fat mayonnaise
+ 3 lettuce leaves
= 1280 kilojoules (306 calories) and 7.5g of fat

g = grams/ tsp = teaspoons

Both of these are good lunch choices, but which one has a lower amount of fat?

What to drink with lunch

Every part of your body needs water to work properly. You need water to sweat when you get too warm. Water keeps your skin smooth and your eyes clean. Your blood is mostly made of water, and it carries **nutrients** to every part of your body.

You need to drink plenty of pure, clean water through the day. You can also make healthy drinks with juices and milk for meals or snack times.

All vegetables have a lot of water and **fibre** in them. Vegetable juice drinks give you lots of vitamins and minerals.

Lunch drinks can be tasty and nutritious. Here is a recipe for a strawberry smoothie. You can make smoothies with nearly any fruit, so try making up your own recipes.

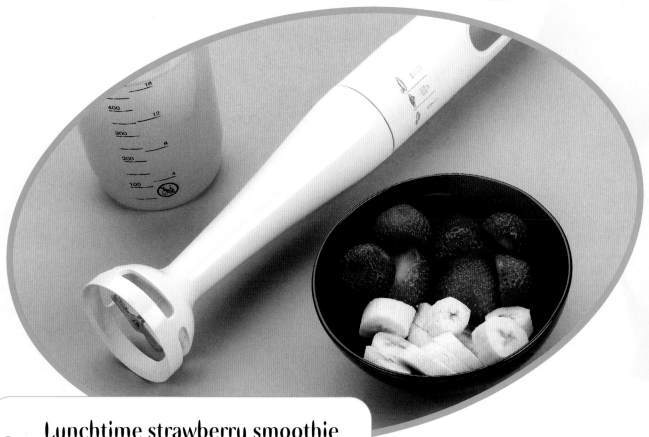

Lunchtime strawberry smoothie

Always ask an adult to help you in the kitchen.

g = grams   ml = millilitres

1. Peel and slice one banana.
2. Place the banana, 275 g frozen strawberries and 150 ml apple juice into a blender, or use a hand mixer.
3. Mix on high speed until smooth and pink.
4. Pour into glasses and enjoy!

23

Prepare a safe lunch

To prepare a safe lunch you must have a clean work surface, free from **germs**. Germs are too tiny to see, but they spoil food and can make you ill. Always wash your hands before you begin. Clean the counter top or work area with a safe disinfectant.

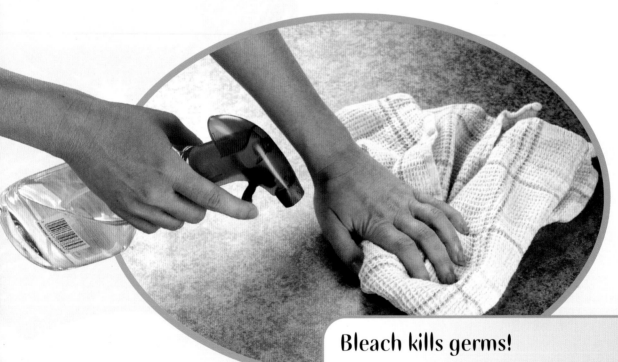

Bleach kills germs!

A solution of bleach and water is safe to use, and kills most germs. Ask an adult to mix one teaspoon of bleach with 500 ml of tap water, and put it in a clean spray bottle. Spray counter tops and wipe clean before and after preparing food.

WARNING: Keep bleach away from your mouth, eyes, and skin.

Make sure that the foods you use to prepare your lunch are safe to eat. The "use by" date on a food label will tell you if food is too old. Don't use food if it looks or smells bad.

Mouldy foods are not safe to eat. If you buy small amounts of fresh food and keep it cold, you can eat it all while it is still fresh.

Packing your lunch

You can pack your own lunch for school, a field trip, or a picnic. Start with your favourite food. Now, use the chart on page 8 to make sure you have foods from each group.

Get ready, get set, pack!

Keep these items at home to help you pack a great lunch!

lunchbox ✔
sandwich bags ✔
flask or juice cartons ✔
serviettes or kitchen paper ✔
small plastic box with lid ✔
plastic spoons and forks ✔
hygenic wipes ✔
your favourite lunch foods ✔

Choose foods carefully for your packed lunches. Foods that don't need to stay cold, like nuts and oranges, will stay safe for many hours. Ask an adult to help you pick good foods to pack.

Easy lunches to pack

Lunchbox 1
cheese and ham sandwich
apple
vegetable sticks
almonds and cashews
bottled water

Lunchbox 2
chicken leg
grapes and banana
tomato
cereal bar
milk in flask

Lunch planner: mini-pizza

preparation time:
20 minutes
cooking time:
10-15 minutes

Most people love pizza! Add your own toppings to this recipe to make your favourite lunch.

You can also use French bread to make great tasting pizza. Just add pizza sauce, vegetables and cheese.

Always ask an adult to help you in the kitchen.

Cooking utensils:
- non-stick baking tray
- chopping board
- sharp knife
- large spatula

Ingredients for each person:
- 1 or 2 pitta breads
- 150 g pizza sauce
- 200 g grated mozerella cheese
- 250 g chopped vegetables – choose three from this list, or your favourites:
  - onions
  - mushrooms
  - red or green pepper
  - spinach leaves
  - sweetcorn

g = grams

Directions:

1. Preheat the oven to 175° C (350° F).

2. Ask an adult to cut the vegetables into small pieces.

3. Place the pitta breads on the baking tray.

4. Spread pizza sauce over the pitta breads.

5. Layer vegetables over the sauce.

6. Sprinkle grated cheese over the vegetables.

7. Cook 10-15 minutes until slightly brown around the edges.

8. While the pizzas cook, set the table with plates, serviettes, cutlery, fresh fruit, and drinks of milk or water.

9. Remove pizzas from the baking tray and place on a chopping board.

10. Cut and serve.

Mini-pizza and fruit is a healthy lunch that you can help prepare. How many vegetables can you see?

Find out for yourself

Choosing foods for a healthy diet is important, but it doesn't have to be difficult. Learn the basic food groups and how much you need from each one. Make good choices and enjoy good health.

Books to read

Look after yourself: Get Some Exercise!, Angela Royston (Heinemann Library, 2004)

Look after yourself: Eat Healthy Food!, Angela Royston (Heinemann Library, 2004)

Go Facts: Healthy Eating, Paul McEvoy (A & C Black, 2005)

Healthy Body Cookbook: Fun Activities and Delicious Recipes for Kids, Joan D'Amico and Karen Eich Drummond (John Wiley & Sons, 1998)

Using the Internet

Explore the Internet to find out more about healthy lunch foods. Websites can change so if some of the links below no longer work, don't worry. Use a search engine, such as **www.yahooligans.com** or **www.internet4kids.com** and type in key words such as "lunch foods," "healthy diet" or "lunch nutrition."

Websites

www.nutrition.org.uk Click on "Education", then "Cook club" for some great recipe ideas.

www.eatwell.gov.uk There is lots of information about diet and health here, as well as quizzes and games.

www.5aday.nhs.uk Find out easy ways to get your 5-a-day, and some delicious smoothie recipes.

Glossary

amino acid part of a protein

carbohydrate the part of food that gives you energy

cell the body's smallest building block of living tissue

cooking utensils the knives, spoons, spatulas, and small tools that you use to prepare food

diet what you usually eat and drink

energy the power needed for your body to work and stay alive

fats a type of nutrient from food that gives you energy

fibre material in foods that is not digested but helps carry the food through the gut

germ a small living organism that can cause disease

gut the parts of your body that your food passes through

immune system the part of your body that protects you from disease and infection

kilojoule a measurement of food energy

lean meat with very little fat

milled ground to make flour

mineral a type of nutrient needed to make the body work correctly

nutrient a substance in food (such as a vitamin, mineral, or protein) that people need to grow and stay healthy

nutrition the part of food that your body can use

protein a type of nutrient in food that gives you energy and is used for growth and repair

vitamin a type of nutrient in food that the body needs to stay healthy and to work correctly

whole grains grains, such as oats, wheat, corn, or rice, that have all or most of their natural fibre and nutrients

Index

Titles in the *What's On Your Plate?* series include:

What's On Your Plate?

Breakfast

Hardback   1 406 20255 X

What's On Your Plate?

Lunch

Hardback   1 406 20256 8

What's On Your Plate?

Dinner

Hardback   1 406 20260 6

What's On Your Plate?

Snacks

Hardback   1 406 20261 4

Find out about the other titles in this series on our website www.raintreepublishers.co.uk